Read-About® Holidays

Passover

By David F. Marx

Consultant
Katharine A. Kane, Reading Specialist
Former Language Arts Coordinator
San Diego County Office of Education

Children's Press®
A Division of Grolier Publishing
New York   London   Hong Kong   Sydney
Danbury, Connecticut

Visit Children's Press® on the Internet at:
http://publishing.grolier.com

Designer: Herman Adler Design Group
Photo Researcher: Caroline Anderson

Library of Congress Cataloging-in-Publication Data

Marx, David F.
    Passover / by David F. Marx.
      p. cm. — (Rookie read-about holidays)
    Includes index.
    Summary: An introduction to the traditions and foods of Passover.
    ISBN 0-516-22214-7 (lib. bdg.)   0-516-27178-4 (pbk.)
    1. Passover—Juvenile literature. [1. Passover. 2. Seder. 3. Holidays.]
  I. Title. II. Series.
  BM695.P3.M37   2001
  296.4'37—dc21
                                      00-029543

Passover is a holiday
celebrated by people
of the Jewish religion.

Passover lasts eight days. The exact dates change from year to year, but Passover always comes in March or April.

April 2001

Sunday	Monday	Tuesday	Wednesday	Thursday	Friday	Saturday
1	2	3	4	5	6	7
8	9	10	11	12	13	14
15	16	17	18	19	20	21
22	23	24	25	26	27	28
29	30					

The dates of Passover are in red on this calendar.

Most Jews celebrate
Passover for only one
or two days.

On these days, families
or larger groups gather
for a Seder (SAY-duhr).

At a Seder, people pray, sing songs, and tell stories. They drink wine or juice and eat special foods. They also serve a huge feast.

Most of the Seder stories are read from a book called the Haggadah (ha-GAH-da).

The word "Haggadah" means "telling."

The Haggadah tells how Jews were slaves long ago in a country called Egypt.

One story is about a man named Moses. Moses helped set the Jews free. He led them out of Egypt.

Moses leads the Jews out of Egypt.

horseradish

lamb bone

egg

parsley

charoset

The Seder foods come from this old, famous story. This is a Seder plate. It holds:

- an egg
- a lamb bone
- parsley
- horseradish
- charoset (cha-RO-set).

Each food has a special meaning on this holiday.

Charoset is a mix of chopped nuts, apples, honey, and cinnamon.

It looks like the same material the Jewish slaves used to make bricks. But it tastes really good!

18

Bite into horseradish.
It is hard to eat because
it tastes so bitter.

Jews eat horseradish to
remember how hard life
was for the Jewish slaves.

Matzo is also served at
a Seder. Matzo is a dry,
flat cracker.

It is a reminder that the Jews
left Egypt in a big hurry.
They did not have time to
let their bread dough rise.

The youngest child at the Seder has a special job. He or she must ask the Four Questions.

These questions are about why Jews do special things on Passover, such as eating the Seder foods.

26

After the meal, the children hunt for a piece of matzo called the afikomen (ah-fee-KO-men).

The afikomen is the last thing Jews eat before leaving the Seder table.

An adult usually hides
the afikomen. The child
who finds it gets a present.

Then the Seder meal
comes to an end.

A child finds the afikomen.

Words You Know

afikomen

charoset

Haggadah

horseradish

30

matzo

Moses

Seder

Seder plate

31

Index

About the Author

David F. Marx is an author and editor of children's books.
He resides in the Chicago area.

Photo Credits

Photographs ©: Corbis-Bettmann: 9 (Roger Ressmeyer), 26, 30 top left (Roger Ressmeyer), 13, 31 top right; Monkmeyer Press: 17, 30 top right (Hershkowitz), 6 (Siteman); Nance S. Trueworthy: cover, 10, 18, 29, 30 bottom right, 30 bottom left; PhotoEdit: 14, 21, 31 bottom right (Bill Aron), 3 (R. Hutchings), 20, 31 top left (Felicia Martinez), 22, 25, 31 bottom left (Michael Newman).